STEP-UP
GEOGRAPHY

The mountain environment

Clare Hibbert

Evans

Published by Evans Brothers Limited
2A Portman Mansions
Chiltern Street
London W1U 6NR

© Evans Brothers Limited 2005

Produced for Evans Brothers Limited by
White-Thomson Publishing Ltd,
Bridgewater Business Centre,
210 High Street,
Lewes, East Sussex BN7 2NH

Printed in China by New Era Printing Co. Ltd

Project manager: Ruth Nason

Designer: Helen Nelson, Jet the Dog

Notes for teachers and parents: Julia Roche

Consultant: John Lace, School Improvement
Manager, Hampshire County Council

Cover: All photographs by Chris Fairclough

British Library Cataloguing in Publication Data

Hibbert, Clare 1970 -

The mountain environment. - (Step-up geography)
1.Mountains - Juvenile literature 2.Mountain
ecology - Juvenile literature

I. Title

551.4'32

ISBN: 0 237 528800

Special thanks to the following for their help and
involvement in the preparation of this book:
St Dominic's School, Harpenden, and Coldean
Primary School, Brighton.

Picture acknowledgements:

Corbis: pages 1/4b (Theo Allofs), 9t (David Samuel
Robbins), 15b (Hal Horwitz), 17l (Tom Brakefield),
18 (John Van Hasselt), 19bl (Anders Ryman), 20c
(Charles E. Rotkin), 20b (John Van Hasselt/Corbis
Sygma), 21 (Jim Zuckerman), 24 (Galen Rowell);
Chris Fairclough: pages 6t, 8t, 12, 26b, 27; Chris
Fairclough Photo Library: pages 4t, 5, 9b, 13, 14,
15t, 19t, 22t, 23t, 26t; Ruth Nason: page 19br;
Helen Nelson: page 7b; Ordnance Survey: page 7t
(Reproduced from Ordnance Survey mapping on
behalf of Her Majesty's Stationery Office © Crown
Copyright 100043633 2004); Papilio: pages 16t
(Steve Austin), 16b (Eric McCabe); Photographers
Direct: pages 10t (Eddie Gerald), 10b (Sylvia
Cordaiy Photo Library), 11 (Kirkendall-Spring
Photographers), 17r (Andrés Morya Photography),
20t (Chris Barton); Science Photo Library: pages 6
(NASA), 25 (Mauro Fermariello); Still Pictures:
pages 22b (A. Riedmiller), 23b (David
Woodfall/WWI).

Maps and diagrams by Helen Nelson.

Contents

Describing mountains 4

Mountains on the map 6

How mountains form 8

Mountain climates 10

Mountains and water 12

Mountain plants 14

Mountain animals 16

Mountain peoples 18

Sacred mountains 20

Tourists 22

Mountain rescue 24

A trip to the mountains 26

Glossary 28

For teachers and parents 30

Index 32

Describing mountains

Have you ever climbed to the top of a mountain? Mountains are steep-sided places that are taller than the land around them. They include the tallest places on the planet. Any mound of land higher than around 600 metres counts as a mountain. Mounds that are not so high are called hills.

▲ The Black Mountains are in Powys, Wales, and their highest point is 811 metres above sea level. Where are the nearest mountains to where you live? Which is the tallest peak?

◄ The world's longest chain of mountains is the Andes. The Andes stretch for 7,240 kilometres along the western coast of South America.

Mountain words

Even if you have never climbed a mountain, you probably have some ideas of what mountains are like. Try to think of as many words as you can that describe the mountain environment, such as 'tall' or 'high'. The mountaintop, or summit, might be 'rocky', 'snowy' or 'windy'. What other words can you think of?

The mountain environment is a special one. The higher you climb, the colder it gets. Some mountains have snowy peaks which stay frozen all year round. The different parts of a mountain provide a habitat for different plants and animals. Some of these are not found in any other kind of place on Earth.

A shape poem

Make up a poem about a mountain. Write it in the shape of a steep-sided mountain and use as many adjectives as you can.

Summit,
Misty, white.
Grotesque face shapes
Peer perpetually from crevasses!
Switchback of paths wind silently up or down.
Majestic scenery at every turn is a feast for the eyes.
Small person on large mountain, I'd like to grow wings and fly.

Different environments

A mountain is not the only kind of special environment. Can you find the names of five types of environment and the description that goes with each?

Dry   Polar   Rainy

Deep   High   Desert

Ocean   Mountain

Icy   Rainforest

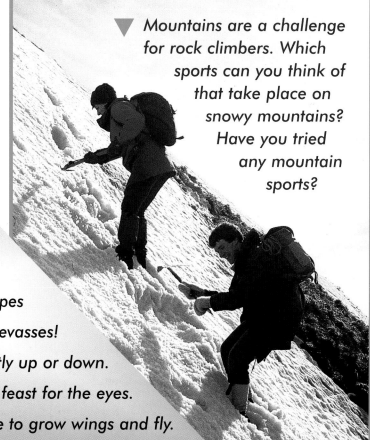

▼ Mountains are a challenge for rock climbers. Which sports can you think of that take place on snowy mountains? Have you tried any mountain sports?

Mountains on the map

Most mountains are part of a group, or range. Mountain ranges are so big that photographs taken on the Earth can show only part of them.

Mountain ranges

Alps	Himalayas
Andes	Queen Maud Range
Appalachians	Rockies
Atlas Mountains	Urals
Great Dividing Range	Virunga Mountains

▲ *See if you can draw in the main mountain ranges on a blank world map.*

There are mountain ranges on all of the seven continents. Ten of them are listed above. Look on a world map or in an atlas and see if you can find them. Make a note of the continent or continents in which you find each range. Which two continents do the Urals stretch across?

◄ *This photo of the Rockies was taken from space – so far away that it includes almost all of the mountain range.*

Continents

Africa
Antarctica
Asia
Australasia
Europe
North America
South America

Map reading

As well as telling us where mountains are, maps give us other information about mountains. On an Ordnance Survey (OS) map, contour lines, colours and shading tell us about the shape and height of the mountain.

Each contour line joins up places that are the same height above sea level. The closer together the contour lines are, the steeper the mountain slope.

▶
▼ *Ben Nevis is the highest mountain in the UK. On the map, the numbers on the contour lines give heights, measured in metres above sea level.*

Compare heights

Ben Nevis is 1,343 metres high. On a map of the British Isles, find the height of three other places – e.g. your home town and some places where you have been on holiday. Make a graph of your findings.

How mountains form

Mountain ranges take millions of years to form. Like many features of the land, they are shaped by movements of the Earth's outer layer, called the crust. The crust is made of giant slabs of rock called plates.

The plates are so big that they carry whole continents or vast areas of ocean. They are moving extremely slowly and, as they move, they sometimes rub against each other, or even crash.

▲ Modelling clay can be used to show how, when two plates crash, the Earth's crust is pushed up into complex folds.

Fold mountains

You can use modelling clay to show what happens when two plates collide. Land on both sides is pushed up. This is how most mountain ranges formed. These kinds of mountains are called fold mountains, because they were made when the land folded up.

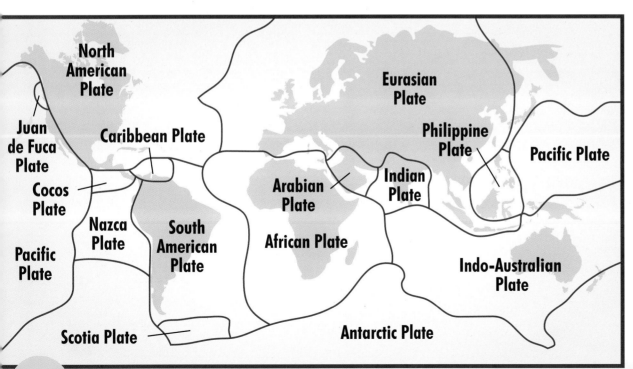

◀ This map shows the plates that make up the Earth's crust. Copy the map and cut along the plate boundaries to make a geographical jigsaw.

North American Plate

Juan de Fuca Plate

Caribbean Plate

Cocos Plate

Nazca Plate

South American Plate

Pacific Plate

Arabian Plate

African Plate

Eurasian Plate

Philippine Plate

Indian Plate

Pacific Plate

Indo-Australian Plate

Scotia Plate

Antarctic Plate

▲ The Himalayas stretch across India, Nepal and Tibet and include the world's ten tallest mountains.

The Himalayas are fold mountains. They formed where the Indian plate crashed into the Eurasian plate. This plate movement is still happening, so the Himalayan mountains are still being pushed up – but only by about a millimetre every year.

▲ Mountain rock is eroded (worn down) by the weather.

Weathering

Something else shapes mountains – the weather. Wind, rain, ice and snow can all wear down mountain rock over time. That is why very old mountains are smoother and lower than younger ones. The wearing down of rock is called erosion.

Other types of mountains

Other types of mountains are dome, fault-block, volcanic and plateau mountains.
Visit http://ia.essortment.com/ mountainmountai_rmky.htm to find out how they are formed.

Mountain climates

When you imagine a mountain, does it have a snowy peak? Most tall mountains do. Above a certain height, known as the snowline, there is always snow, even in summer.

The climate of a place is its average weather over a period of time – for example, its temperature and rainfall. The mountain environment does not have one climate. On a mountain, the climate changes the higher up you go. The temperature drops by about 1 degree Centigrade for every 150 metres that you climb.

▲ *The photographs on these two pages show a mountain called the Matterhorn in the Swiss Alps, in winter (above), spring (below) and summer (page 11). What are the differences between them?*

A mountain poster

You could research a particular mountain and find out about the average weather there in different seasons. Then make a poster with four pictures, each showing the mountain in a different season.

You could use symbols like these to denote each season's weather.

 Cloudy

 Snow

 Rain

Sunny

 Risk of flooding

 Warm

 Cold

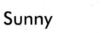 Windy

Seasons

The weather on mountains near the Equator does not change very much. Further north or south, mountains have seasons. Winter is long and cold, with blizzards. The strong winds can blow the snow into snowdrifts, which may be several metres high. In spring, when the warmth of the Sun melts most of the snow, streams overflow and there may be flooding. Sometimes melting snow can cause avalanches. Summer is short and stormy. Autumn is chilly and foggy.

▶ *There are hundreds of lakes in the Alps. Holiday brochures for this type of landscape are often called 'Lakes and Mountains'.*

Mountains and water

Mountains are so big that they affect the water cycle. Clouds that blow in from the sea cool over mountains and the water falls as rain.

Because the wind blows clouds from the sea across land, rain falls on the side of mountains that is closest to the coast. The other side is in a rain shadow. It is drier, because few rain clouds reach it. Much of North and South America is in rain shadow, because the Rocky Mountains and the Andes block moist air from the Pacific Ocean.

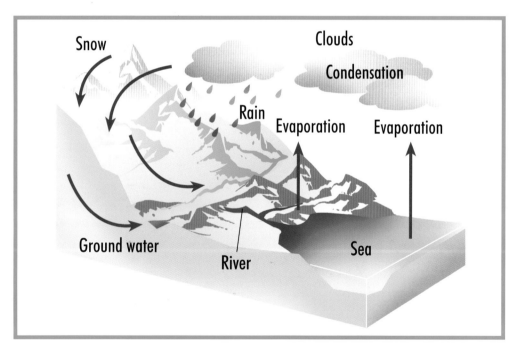

▲ In the water cycle, heat from the Sun causes sea water to evaporate. The water vapour rises and condenses to form clouds, which are blown in to land. As the clouds are blown higher, they cool and the water falls as rain or snow.

Rainfall

In an atlas, find a map showing rainfall in the British Isles. Describe where you see the areas of greatest rainfall and say why you think the most rain falls there.

Streams and rivers

When rainwater falls on mountains, it fills mountain streams, which later grow into rivers. Rain also seeps into the layers between the rocks, eventually bubbling out as a mountain spring.

People who live in the mountains take the fresh water they need from mountain streams and rivers, and so it is important that the water is not polluted. However, other human needs can conflict with this. For example, mining brings much-needed money to mountain peoples, but it can pollute mountain streams, leaving the water dangerous to drink.

Water and trees

Rainwater can rush down a mountain slope, taking the soil with it, but this does not happen where trees are growing. The trees hold the water in their roots. Can you explain why cutting down trees would cause problems for mountain people?

Frozen waters

Vast areas of mountains are covered in ice. There are slow-moving rivers of ice, called glaciers, and layers of ice, known as ice sheets or ice caps. Glaciers play a part in shaping the land, just as ordinary rivers do. Melting glaciers may also feed mountain rivers.

▼ *Global warming is shrinking some glaciers like this one in the Rockies. Fast-melting glaciers can cause floods or landslides.*

Mountain plants

You have seen how the climate changes from the lowlands to the top of a mountain. The types of plant that grow on mountains change in the same way.

Think about the harsh conditions that plants must survive high in the mountains. As well as the low temperatures, there is thin, poor soil, which is often frozen. Plants growing in rain shadow also cope with little water.

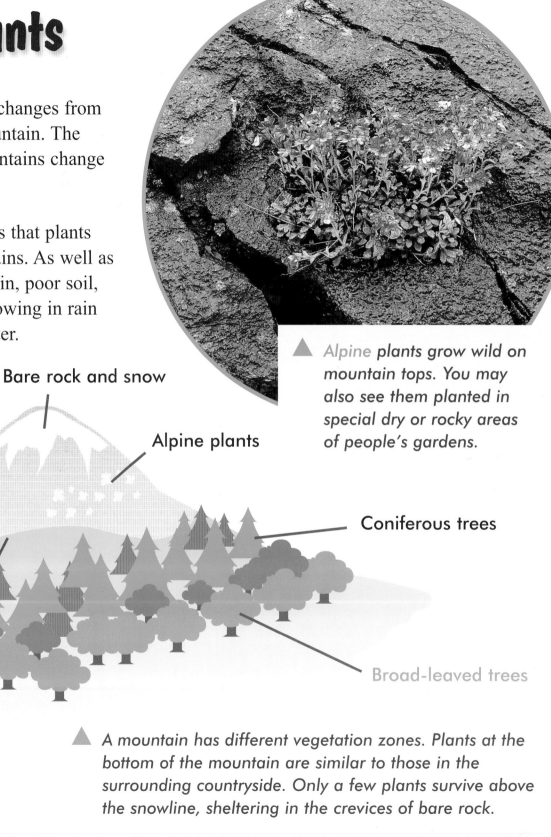

Alpine plants grow wild on mountain tops. You may also see them planted in special dry or rocky areas of people's gardens.

Bare rock and snow

Snowline

Alpine plants

Coniferous trees

Broad-leaved trees

Tree line (no trees grow above this level)

A mountain has different vegetation zones. Plants at the bottom of the mountain are similar to those in the surrounding countryside. Only a few plants survive above the snowline, sheltering in the crevices of bare rock.

Tree types

From the diagram on page 14, you can see that there are broad-leaved trees on the lower slopes. Higher up, these give way to evergreen trees called conifers. Their tough, needle-shaped leaves do not dry out in the wind. The trees' cone shape means that snow slides off the branches instead of piling up and breaking them.

Alpines

Alpine plants are found above the tree line, where there are no trees to provide shelter. They grow in rounded clumps close to the ground, so they cannot be flattened by fierce winds or heavy snows.

Unique plants

Mountains are home to amazing plant life. This includes food plants, such as the mountain blueberry, medicinal plants like mountain mint, and rare lichens and mosses.

▲ Mountains are carpeted with brightly-coloured flowers for a few short weeks each spring.

◄ Mountain mint is a medicinal plant which grows across North America. Its crushed flowers are a traditional remedy for toothache.

Mini mountain

As a class, design a rockery which you could offer to build for a nearby hospital or care home. Rocks, sand and gritty compost could be used to mimic the poor soil above the tree line.

15

Mountain animals

Similar kinds of animals live on all mountains. These are animals that are well adapted to the mountain environment.

Small, furry animals can cope well with the cold. Perhaps you have a mountain animal as a pet. Rabbits, guinea pigs, chinchillas and marmots all live in burrows. They feed on scrubby mountain grasses.

▲ *The mountain hare lives in a dip in the ground, but in very severe weather it digs a burrow. The hare's fur turns white each winter, as* camouflage *against the snow.*

Larger mountain animals need to be sure-footed to cope with steep slopes. They include sheep, goats, elk, yaks and llamas. Their hooves can dig into loose soil, snow or scree for grip.

◀ *What features of this llama are designed for life in the Andes mountains? How do hooves and thick, waterproof wool help?*

Mountain predators

Animals that hunt other animals for food are called predators. Only a few can survive on any mountain, because food is scarce. Snow leopards are predators in the Himalayas, and pumas hunt in mountains across North and South America.

Birds of prey glide around the upper slopes. Eagles can kill prey as large as sheep with their curved talons. Condors, a type of vulture, swoop down to feed on animals that are already dead.

▼ *Pumas have over forty different names. 'Mountain lion' is one. Can you find out any others?*

Animals in danger

Many mountain animals are endangered. Mountain gorillas live in the cloud forests of eastern Central Africa. Their forests are being cut down, and they are also killed by poachers. Look on the internet to find campaigns to save endangered animals such as the mountain gorilla.

◀ *The Andean condor has the widest wingspan of any bird. Outstretched, its wings measure three metres across.*

Plotting populations

Use the internet to find out the populations of some mountain animals now, and around 50 years ago. With this data, produce a pictograph showing the decline (or rise) of different mountain animals.

Mountain peoples

Mountains are beautiful, wild places, but the climate and many other features make it difficult to live there.

Thin air

We all need to breathe in oxygen from the air to stay alive, but high in the mountains the air contains less oxygen than air in the lowlands. Mountain people have adapted to this thin air. They may have larger lungs, which can take in more air, and bigger hearts, which can pump more oxygen-carrying blood.

Communication and supplies

Mountains may not have proper roads and this makes it hard for people living in the mountains to travel to schools or hospitals in the lowlands.

Many mountain communities are not reached by power lines and piped water and so people must make their own light and heat and collect their own water. They need to do this without damaging the fragile mountain environment. Some burn animal dung as fuel, instead of chopping down precious trees.

▲ *Sherpa* **people live in the Himalayas. Like Apa Sherpa, the father of this family, many Sherpas work as guides for climbers. Apa Sherpa has climbed to the top of Everest twelve times.**

Historic diary

Sherpa guide Tenzing Norgay was the first to reach the summit of Everest, along with New Zealander Edmund Hillary. Use the internet to find out about the expedition. Then write Norgay's diary of the last stage of the climb.

Making a living

Many mountain people live off the land. They grow crops on the lower slopes and take their animals to the higher slopes to graze each summer. Some mountain people make a living from mining and others make money from tourism. They guide climbers and trekkers or sell handicrafts, such as woven blankets.

▲ In the Andes, some people mine metal ores, which are found deep within the mountain.

▲ A difficulty for mountain farmers is that rain can wash away the soil and young plants growing in sloping fields. To prevent this, many farmers cut terraces like these rice fields in Bali.

▼ This French herder is leading her cows down from high pastures. Traditionally, farmers graze their cows, sheep and horses on the high slopes between May and October.

Sacred mountains

In many cultures, mountains are special, holy places. Can you think why?

▼ *Mount Fuji, Japan, is a sacred place for followers of Shinto and Buddhism. Around 200,000 pilgrims from these two religions climb to the top of Fuji each summer.*

▲ *Mount Olympus was thought to be the home of the ancient Greek gods.*

▼ *To Australia's Aboriginal peoples, Uluru represents a snake spirit, the mother and father of every living thing.*

A high mountain is very mysterious. Its peak is sometimes hidden by cloud. It is a place where the Earth meets the heavens. That is why people imagined that gods and spirits lived on mountains.

Sacred story

Write a story about good and evil, set on a sacred mountain.

Home of the gods

The ancient Greeks said that their supreme god, Zeus, lived on Mount Olympus, along with all the other gods and goddesses. Can you guess which sporting event, originally held to honour Zeus, is named after Mount Olympus?

The ancient Chinese thought that mountains were pillars holding up the heavens. Later, they named five sacred peaks. These were home to the immortals – spirits that lived forever.

The Kikuyu people of Kenya believe that their god, Ngai, lives in the clouds on top of Mount Kenya. They traditionally build their homes with the doors facing the mountain.

Mountains in the Bible

There are many stories about mountains in the Bible. Mount Sinai was where God gave Moses the Ten Commandments. Jesus rose into heaven from the Mount of Olives.

Places of worship

Some temples are built in the shape of mountains. They include the pyramids of the Maya, ziggurats built in ancient Mesopotamia, and stupas and pagodas built in Asia.

▼ These temple ruins on top of Machu Picchu, a peak in the Andes, were built by the Inca people around 600 years ago.

Tourists

Many people visit mountains as tourists, to experience the beauty of the mountain environment and to take part in mountain activities.

As well as skiing, hiking and climbing, there is fishing in mountain streams and rivers and plenty of wildlife to watch. See if you can find pictures of different mountain activities. Which season would be best for each one?

▶ *Skiers come to the mountains when the slopes are covered in snow. Ski resorts attract businesses to the mountains, including shops, hotels and restaurants.*

◀ *Paragliding is a sport where people jump from a mountain, wearing a special parachute. They can enjoy the view and the feeling of flying as they drift safely to the ground below.*

Tourist leaflet

Write and design a leaflet to attract tourists to a mountain environment, such as Yellowstone or the Canadian Rockies. What activities can they enjoy? What animals and plants might they see? Include a table or graph to show the weather in different seasons. Use the internet to research the information.

Changing the land

When people visit a place, they have an effect on it. Can you think how tourists change the mountain environment? All visitors to a mountain help to wear it away with their footsteps, and some leave litter behind. However, holidaymakers also bring money to the region when they pay to stay in guesthouses or employ local people as guides.

▶ *Walkers wear away the land of the mountain, causing erosion. In some places, this eventually loosens the rocks and causes a mini landslide.*

◀ *How would you stop people dropping litter on mountains? Why do you think some people do not want litter bins or 'No litter' signs?*

For and against

Have a debate to see if you think tourists are mostly good or mostly bad for the mountain environment. You could draw up an action plan of ways to stop tourists from damaging mountains, such as limiting the number of visitors.

Mountain rescue

Each year, climbers, hikers and other mountain tourists get into difficulties. You may have heard news stories about amazing mountain rescues. You can find information on the internet, too.

Being lost on a mountain is dangerous. If people stay at low temperatures for too long, their bodies stop working properly. This is called hypothermia and can cause death. Frostbite is another danger, when fingers, toes or noses freeze solid.

On very high slopes, people can get mountain sickness because of the lack of oxygen. The first signs are feeling sick and giddy. Later, the person might go into a coma or even die.

◀ *This rescue helicopter is pulling some climbers to safety. Helicopters are the best vehicles for reaching out-of-the-way places.*

▶ *The weather on a mountain can change quickly. Clouds reduce visibility, and this is dangerous for hikers and climbers.*

Search and rescue

When people go missing in the mountains, search parties look for them. Helicopters and aircraft can cover a big area and reach remote peaks, but they cost a lot of money. Usually rescue workers go out on foot or on skis, helped by teams of trained dogs. They often risk their own lives.

Avoiding danger

Can you think of measures that would help to reduce the number of people needing to be rescued? For example, some mountains have storm shelters. Climbers can also carry mobile phones and GPS (Global Positioning System) devices.

◀ *Dogs are often used for rescue work, because of their brilliant senses of hearing and smell.*

Newspaper article

Write a newspaper article expressing one of these opinions:

a) Rescue workers should not have to risk their lives and waste resources rescuing climbers.

b) People have a right to climb mountains – and a right to be rescued if they get into difficulties.

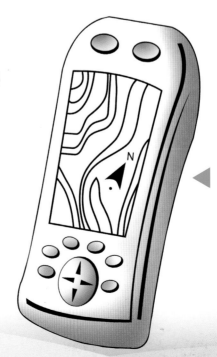

◀ *GPS receivers like this pick up signals from special satellites in space, showing users their exact position.*

A trip to the mountains

Think about the preparations you would need to make for a trip to the mountains.

You would need to be sure that you were fit. Real mountaineers do months of fitness training before they go on an expedition.

To plan your route, you would need to use a detailed map and also find out if there are areas that you need to avoid. This may mean areas of danger, such as where there is a risk of landslides, or places where there are fragile mountain plants.

▶ *It's important to check the weather forecast before a mountain expedition. You can find a forecast for your area on the Met Office website. There is also information there about mountain weather and safety.*

▲ *If you go hiking in the mountains, always go with someone experienced. Tell someone where you are going and when you will be back, so that they can send out a search party if you do not return.*

Emergency alphabet

If you know this alphabet, you can spell out where you are to someone on the phone and never be misunderstood.

A   Alpha
B   Bravo
C   Charlie
D   Delta
E   Echo
F   Foxtrot
G   Golf
H   Hotel
I   India
J   Juliet
K   Kilo
L   Lima
M   Mike
N   November
O   Oscar
P   Papa
Q   Quebec
R   Romeo
S   Sierra
T   Tango
U   Uniform
V   Victor
W   Whiskey
X   X-ray
Y   Yankee
Z   Zulu

▲ *Prepare for any emergency, but remember that you have to carry your kit.*

What to wear

You would need good walking boots and a hat to keep off the sun and rain. Jeans are not suitable, because if they get wet, they take a long time to dry and are uncomfortable. It is best to wear layers of light clothing under a waterproof jacket and trousers, and to carry some spare clothes, too.

What to take

In your backpack you would need water, food and a map. In case of emergency you should take a first aid kit, mobile phone, torch, distress flares and a whistle.

If you are well prepared you should not get into difficulties – but on the mountains, anything can happen! So practise making the international distress signal with a torch or whistle: six flashes or whistles followed by a one-minute gap, then six flashes or whistles again.

▶ *A whistle is good for emergencies, but can only be heard for a short distance. How else could you signal for help?*

Glossary

alpine | a plant that grows above the tree line.

avalanche | a sudden fall of lots of snow down a mountain.

blizzard | a snowstorm with very strong winds.

broad-leaved tree | a tree that has broad leaves, which it loses in winter.

Buddhism | a religion based on the teachings of the Buddha, who lived around 2,500 years ago.

camouflage | a way of blending into the background.

climate | the average weather of a place over a period of time.

cloud forest | a tropical rainforest on or near mountains.

conifer | a tree that has needle-shaped leaves which it never loses all at once.

continent | one of the seven great land masses on Earth.

contour line | an imaginary line on the ground that joins together places that are the same height above sea level.

crust | the solid layer of rock on the surface of the Earth.

decline | fall in numbers.

distress flare | a firework that can be set off to send a streak of light into the sky, to draw attention from a rescue party.

endangered | in danger of dying out.

environment | surroundings or landscape.

Equator | an imaginary line around the centre of the Earth. It is the hottest part of Earth's surface, the part furthest away from the poles.

erosion | the wearing away of rock.

fragile | easily damaged.

frostbite | when body parts freeze. If they are not treated quickly, the flesh dies and must be cut away.

glacier | a large, slow-moving river of ice (or ice and rock).

global warming | the warming of the Earth caused by gases that stop heat escaping from Earth's atmosphere.

GPS (Global Positioning System) | a system that allows people to pinpoint their exact position on Earth (the globe), using a device that picks up radio signals from satellites in space.

habitat | the place where a plant or animal lives.

hypothermia | when someone's body temperature drops so low that the body's organs no longer work properly.

ice cap | the ice-covered top of a mountain.

ice sheet | a thick sheet of ice covering a large area of land.

immortal | someone who lives forever.

Inca | Indian people who lived in the Andes mountains and established a great empire, between the 1200s and 1400s.

landslide | soil or rocks sliding down a mountain.

medicinal	can be used as medicine, to treat disease, sickness or pain.	**sacred**	holy and special.
Met Office	government department that monitors the UK's weather and gives forecasts.	**Sherpa**	an Eastern Tibetan people who live in the Himalayas.
mining	digging coal, metals or other minerals out of the ground.	**Shinto**	the ancient religion of Japan, which holds that kami (gods) are present in every living thing.
mountaineer	someone who climbs mountains.	**snowdrift**	a bank of snow that has been blown by the wind.
mountain sickness	when a person becomes ill high in the mountains because of lack of oxygen.	**snowline**	level beyond which a mountain is permanently covered in snow.
Ordnance Survey (OS)	mapping agency which makes detailed maps of every area of the United Kingdom.	**spring**	a place where rainwater trickles or bubbles out of the ground.
oxygen	gas found in air which all animals need to breathe to survive.	**stupa**	a dome-shaped Buddhist shrine, or holy place.
pagoda	a multi-storeyed Buddhist temple.	**summit**	the very top of a mountain.
peak	the pointed top of a mountain.	**talon**	a curved claw.
pilgrim	someone who makes a journey to a sacred place.	**terrace**	level areas of land, cut into a mountain slope.
plate	one of the giant slabs of rock that make up the Earth's crust or surface.	**tree line**	level beyond which no trees grow on a mountain, because it is too cold.
poacher	a person who illegally hunts animals for food or to sell.	**water cycle**	the natural cycle of water on Earth. Water falls to the Earth as rain, which fills streams and rivers and flows into the oceans. Ocean water heated by the Sun rises in the air as water vapour to form clouds, which later cool and allow the water to fall back to Earth as rain.
pollute	to make the air, water or earth dirty or poisonous.		
predator	an animal that hunts other animals for food.		
prey	an animal that is hunted by other animals for food.		
pyramid	a building with a square base and sloping, triangular sides.	**ziggurat**	a Babylonian temple shaped like a steep pyramid with stepped sides. The Babylonians lived in ancient Mesopotamia (present-day Iraq) between 4,000 and 2,500 years ago.
rain shadow	region on the side of a mountain which faces away from the coast or incoming winds and receives little rainfall.		
range	a group of mountains.		

For teachers and parents

This book is designed to support and extend the learning objectives of Unit 15 of the QCA Geography Scheme of Work. Its information and activities and the suggestions below will help you to support children's learning about:

- weather, including microclimates, seasons and world weather
- settlement: land use issues
- environment: impact and sustainability

and to help children develop the following skills:

- observing and questioning
- collecting and recording evidence
- analysing and communicating
- using geographical vocabulary
- using globes and atlases
- identifying places on maps
- using secondary sources
- using ICT

The Scheme of Work suggests that children research and compare three different mountain environments, one within the British Isles. The notes below suggest how this could be done, as you work with this book, using the Cairngorms, the Andes and the Himalayas.

SUGGESTED FURTHER ACTIVITIES

Pages 4-5 Describing mountains
Using atlases and then globes, find South America and identify the Andes mountains. Ask the children to work with a partner to name the countries through which the Andes stretch.

Discuss lines of longitude and latitude and their numbering, especially the Equator and the Tropics of Cancer and Capricorn. You might also refer to Longitude 0, the Greenwich Meridian, and its importance in measuring time worldwide.

The children could be asked to research equatorial and tropical climates. A child-friendly website is:
http://www.ace.mmu.ac.uk/eae/Climate/Younger/Climate_Zones.html

Pages 6-7 Mountains on the map
In the children's atlases, find a map of the world showing physical features. Give the children the map reference for the Himalayas (27N to 30N and 78E to 98E) and ask them which mountains they find there.

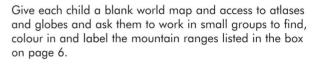

Give each child a blank world map and access to atlases and globes and ask them to work in small groups to find, colour in and label the mountain ranges listed in the box on page 6.

The activity box on page 7 asks the children to make a graph of their findings. This will be a block graph showing the comparative heights of four places. Some Maths work on converting feet to metres would be helpful before beginning this work. There is a table showing heights in both feet and metres at:
http://www.udel.edu/interlit/images/20tables/highest.htm

You will find some helpful ideas at:http://www.newton.mec.edu/ Angier/DimSum/Mt.%20Everest%20Lesson.html. There are some beautiful photographs and a link to mountain poems.

Pages 8-9 How mountains form
It would be helpful to enlarge the plates map to A4, before copying it for the children to work on the jigsaw. You could possibly erase the names of the smaller plates and rewrite them so that they fit inside the appropriate areas.

You might like to try making a fault-block mountain using differently shaped wooden blocks from a child's set.

Dome, volcanic and plateau mountains could be demonstrated by using newspaper scrunched into shape and then covered with Mod-Roc or similar (plaster of Paris type material).

Pages 10-11 Mountain climates
You might like to divide the class into three groups to research climatic conditions in three different mountain ranges, such as the Cairngorms, the Andes and the Himalayas. Within their groups the children could work in pairs to use the internet or reference books. Some useful websites are:

http://www.travel-himalayas.com/about-himalayas/climate-himalaya.html

http://www.cairngormmountain.com

http://www.blueplanetbiomes.org/andes.htm

Pages 12-13 Mountains and water
When describing the areas of greatest rainfall (page 12), the children should be encouraged to use compass points to pinpoint areas in the country and to give names of any mountain ranges involved.

Discuss the windward (facing the prevailing wind) and lee of mountains and how this causes a rain shadow. Link these ideas to the children's findings.

http://www.mountainpartnership.org/themes/themes.html talks about a voluntary group with representatives from all over the world, which works to improve the lives of mountain people and protect mountain environments. It includes a link to water.

Pages 14-15 Mountain plants

If you can find a copy of *The Atlas of World Wildlife* (Mitchell Beazley, 1973), it will be invaluable in these researches. It is beautifully illustrated throughout. On page 112 it gives a great description of life on the roof of the world; how it arrived and survives there.

You could, perhaps, use the same three-group organisation as suggested for pages 10-11, to explore the plant life of the three mountain environments already described. Begin to build up a classroom display about these three environments, using the flags of the different countries involved.

Pages 16-17 Mountain animals

Children could work in the same three groups as before and change partners or not as you think best.

www.blueplanetbiomes.org/andes.htm has a good introductory section dealing with facts about the height and length of the Andes and good links for information on plants, birds and animals.

Go to www.travel-himalayas.com/national-parks-sanctuaries and click on 'The Great Himalayan National Park', which is a high-altitude wildlife reserve. This site has lots of information on indigenous flora and fauna and the children could select some for further research and prepare work to add to the display. The written work could be enhanced with the children's drawings and paintings.

The Cairngorms site from pages 10-11 can be used again for this work. *The Atlas of World Wildlife* has excellent text and illustrations of life above the snowline.

Pages 18-19 Mountain peoples

To help the children with their diaries of the final stages of Tenzing Norgay's climb, visit http://www.nationalgeographic.com/everest/ and go to the 'Kids' section where you will be able to take part in a virtual climb. You may find this rather slow to download, but it is well worth the wait.

There is also a site where you can find interviews with over 300 people who live in highland and mountainous regions all over the world: http://www.mountainvoices.org. It includes excellent photographs of the people being interviewed.

Pages 20-21 Sacred mountains

http://www.mountainpartnership.org/themes/themes.html has a link to Sacred mountains. It addresses the environmental issues raised by steady streams of pilgrims and also steady streams of tourists. This will be helpful for the next page also.

Pages 22-23 Tourists

Most of the websites mentioned so far have information about tourism and the activities that are available to visitors. Children will find lots of ideas for their leaflets and should again work on one of the three mountainous regions already chosen. Some sites also talk about the environmental issues raised by encouraging large numbers of visitors to an area.

This would be a good opportunity to make a link with Science work on Rocks and Soil. It is sometimes possible to borrow a box of rock samples from your local teacher's resources centre or museum. You could investigate rock types and test each sample for hardness or resistance to erosion. The children could use ICT to record their results.

Visit http://www.seafriends.org.nz/enviro/soil. This site lists the different types of rock and links for further information. Although some of the information is much more than is needed here, the introduction to each rock type is very good.

Pages 24-25 Mountain rescue

http://www.mountain.rescue.org.uk/home.html deals with mountain rescue in England and Wales and has excellent sections on 'Mountain Advice' and 'Funding', the latter dealing with the kind of issues that the children are asked to explore in their newspaper articles. There were no stories of real rescues and I think you and the children would have to search newspapers for these events which, fortunately, do not appear in the news too often. You might ask your local library or teacher's library if they have any fictional stories involving mountain rescue.

Pages 26-27 A trip to the mountains

The website given for the previous page will also be useful here when talking about preparing for a trip.

The Met Office site, http://www.met-office.gov.uk, gives weather forecasts for all regions of the UK and there is general information about mountain weather and safety. Click on 'Mountain weather' for information about obtaining bespoke weather forecasts by fax, for the Eastern and Western Highlands, Snowdonia and the Lake District.

There might be some opportunities here for dance/drama activities. Or groups of children could work out some role-play situations, having practised their emergency drills.

If you have suitable outdoor areas you could try some simple orienteering using Silva compasses and a plan. It can be fun to do, using laminated pictures cut into jigsaw-shaped pieces hung in different parts of the school grounds. Use a different picture for each of five or six groups and identify the pieces of each group's picture with a letter and a number: e.g. A1, A2, A3. This activity can be made competitive, if you wish, by adding in a time factor.

It is possible to do some preliminary orienteering work in the classroom. You will find helpful ideas in your QCA Physical Education folder. Unit 3, Outdoor and adventurous activities, covers orienteering at year 5/6 level.

The REM catalogue at http://www.r-e-m.co.uk contains some CD Roms which could be useful for this work. Heinemann *Explore Analysing Data* has one called *Landscapes* which explores key features of mountain environments, forests, deserts and polar regions. The activities encourage analysis, communication and presentation of data. Granada Learning has a CD Rom called *Exploring maps* which has some excellent activities for developing concepts of maps and mapping. Both of the above are aimed at ages 7 to 11.

Presentation

When all the information and data on the three mountain areas have been collected, each of the three groups should arrange a presentation for the class. They should use a variety of methods of communicating their findings, e.g. whiteboard, power point, graphs, overhead projector and own-design leaflets or posters.

Index

air 18
alpines 14, 15
Alps 6, 10, 11
ancient Chinese 21
ancient Greeks 20, 21
Andes 4, 6, 12, 19, 21
animals 5, 16, 17, 19, 22
Appalachians 6
Asia 6, 21
Atlas Mountains 6
Australia 20
avalanches 11

Ben Nevis 7
Bible 21
birds 17
Black Mountains 4
blizzards 11

climate 10, 14, 18
clothes 27
cloud forests 17
condors 17
conifers 15
continents 6, 8
contour lines 7
crust 8

dogs 25

eagles 17
emergencies 27
endangered animals 17
environment 5, 18, 22, 23
Equator 11
erosion 9
Everest 18

farmers 19
flowers 15
fold mountains 8, 9

glaciers 13
global warming 13
gods 20, 21
GPS 25
Great Dividing Range 6

habitat 5
hearts 18
height of mountains 7
helicopters 24, 25
Hillary, Edmund 18
hills 4
Himalayas 6, 9, 17, 18
holidays 11

ice caps 13
ice sheets 13
Incas 21
India 9

Japan 20

Kenya 21

lakes 11
landslides 13, 23, 26
litter 23
llamas 16
lungs 18

Machu Picchu 21
maps 6, 7, 26, 27
Matterhorn 10, 11
mining 13, 19
mobile phones 25, 27

mountain activities 22
mountain gorilla 17
mountain hare 16
mountain sickness 24
Mount Fuji 20
Mount Kenya 21
Mount Olympus 20, 21
Mount Sinai 21

Norgay, Tenzing 18
North America 6, 12, 15, 17

Ordnance Survey 7
oxygen 18, 24

peak 4, 5, 10, 20, 21, 25
plants 5, 14, 15, 22, 26
plates 8, 9
pollution 13
power lines 18
pumas 17

Queen Maud Range 6

rain 9, 11, 12, 13, 19, 27
rainfall 10, 12
rain shadow 12, 14
ranges 6, 8
religions 20
rescue workers 25
rivers 13, 22
roads 18
Rockies 6, 12, 13, 22

seasons 11
shape of mountains 7

Sherpas 18
skiing 22
snow 9, 10, 11, 12, 14, 15, 16, 22
snowdrifts 11
snow leopards 17
snowline 10, 14
soil 13, 14, 15, 19
South America 4, 6, 12, 17
spring (water) 13
storm shelters 25
streams 11, 13, 22
summit 5, 18

temperature 10, 14, 24
temples 21
terraces 19
tourism 19, 22
tourists 22, 23, 24
tree line 14, 15
trees 13, 14
types of mountains 9

Uluru 20
Urals 6

vegetation zones 14
Virunga Mountains 6

water 12, 13, 14, 18
water cycle 12
weather 9, 10, 11, 22, 24, 26
weathering 9
wind 9, 11, 12, 15

Yellowstone 22